HAL LEONARD PIANO REPERTOIRE
Book 2 • *Late Elementary*

JOURNEY THROUGH THE
CLASSICS

COMPILED, EDITED, AND RECORDED BY JENNIFER LINN

Dedicated in loving memory to my mother and first teacher,
Geraldine Ruth Ryan Lange.

To access recorded performances online, visit:
www.halleonard.com/mylibrary

Enter Code
6801-5014-5697-4534

Cover Art: Rose Garden, 1876 (oil on canvas) by Claude Monet (1840-1926)
Private Collection/ Photo © Lefevre Fine Art Ltd., London/ The Bridgeman Art Library
Nationality / copyright status: French / out of copyright
Adaptation by Jen McClellan

ISBN 978-1-4950-1314-0

7777 W. BLUEMOUND RD. P.O. BOX 13819 MILWAUKEE, WI 53213

In Australia Contact:
Hal Leonard Australia Pty. Ltd.
4 Lentara Court
Cheltenham, Victoria, 3192 Australia
Email: ausadmin@halleonard.com.au

Visit Hal Leonard Online at
www.halleonard.com

JOURNEY THROUGH THE CLASSICS:
Book 2 Reference Chart

WHEN COMPLETED	PAGE	TITLE	COMPOSER	ERA	KEY	METER	CHALLENGE ELEMENTS
	4	Russian Folk Song	Beethoven	Classical	G	2/4	Dotted rhythm; legato/staccato coordination
	5	Sonatina in C	Duncombe	Baroque	C	2/4	Triplet and duplet rhythms; RH finger substitution
	6	Minuet in G	Telemann	Baroque	G	3/4	Triplet and duplet rhythms; portato touch
	7	Menuet in F	Mozart, L.	Classical	F	3/4	Hand shifts; LH octaves; echo dynamics
	8	Trumpet Tune	Duncombe	Baroque	C	3/4	Repeated notes and harmonic thirds; hand position extension
	10	Waltz	Vogel	Romantic	G	3/4	Balance between melody & accompaniment; connecting pedal
	12	Little Sonata	Wilton	Classical	C	4/4 & 3/4	Accents; syncopation; echo dynamics; RH/LH coordination
	14	Melody (Arabian Air)	Le Couppey	Romantic	Am	2/4	Legato touch; phrasing; 16th notes; fermata
	16	Minuet in G	Bach, J.S.	Baroque	G	3/4	Articulation; contrapuntal skills; crossing 3 over 1
	18	Morning Prayer	Gurlitt	Romantic	C	¢	Vertical reading; Connecting pedal; both hands in 𝄞
	20	Bagatelle	Diabelli	Classical	C	3/8	3/8 time signature; balance between melody & accompaniment
	21	Tarantella	Lynes	Romantic	Am	6/8	6/8 time signature; fast legato scales in RH/staccato in LH
	22	Giga	Arnold	Classical	C	6/8	Fast and continuous scale patterns in RH
	24	Musette	Le Couppey	Romantic	G	¢	Drone bass; articulation; RH scale patterns with finger crossings
	26	Scotch Dance	Kuhlau	Classical	C	2/4	Alberti bass; sforzando chords; coordination between hands
	27	Burleske	Mozart, L.	Classical	G	2/4	Broken LH octaves; 16th notes; articulation
	28	Menuet in G	Petzold	Baroque	G	3/4	Articulation; finger crossing and contrapuntal skills
	30	Menuet in F	Mozart, W.A.	Classical	F	3/4	Finger substitution; articulation; triplet rhythm
	32	Church Bells	Camidge	Classical	C	2/4	Vertical reading; connecting pedal; both hands in 𝄞
	33	Bright Sky	Gurlitt	Romantic	C	2/4	Alberti bass with shifts; both hands in 𝄞; repeated notes
	36	Sad at Heart	Fuchs	Romantic	Am	3/4	Phrasing and balance; pedal; voicing; expression
	37	Sarabande	Pachelbel	Baroque	B♭	4/4	B-flat Key signature; vertical reading; connecting pedal
	38	Distant Bells	Streabbog	Romantic	C	4/4	Crossing LH over RH; connecting pedal; accents; balance
	40	Night Escape	Gurlitt	Romantic	Dm	4/4	LH melody with RH repeating harmonic seconds and thirds

CONTENTS

Russian Folk Song

Ludwig van Beethoven
(1770–1827)

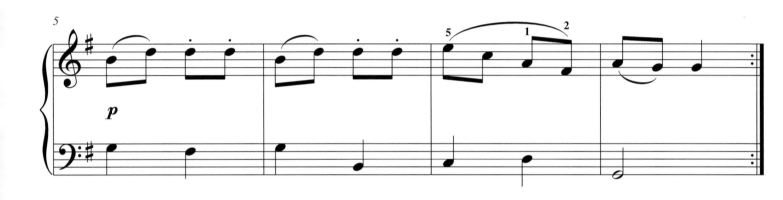

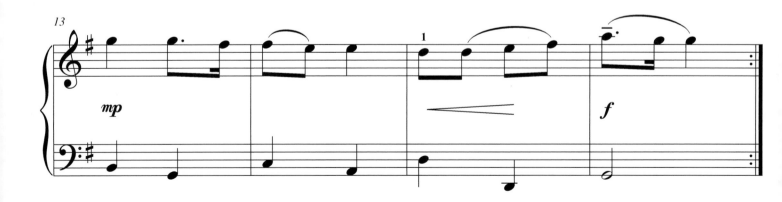

Sonatina in C Major

William Duncombe
(1690–1769)

Minuet in G Major

Georg Philipp Telemann
(1681–1767)

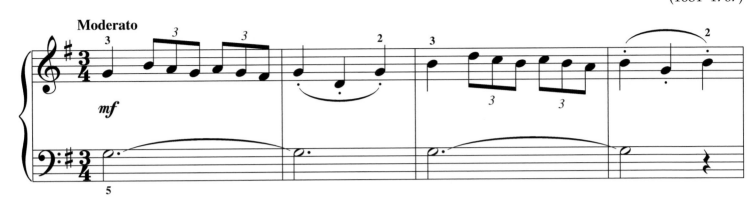

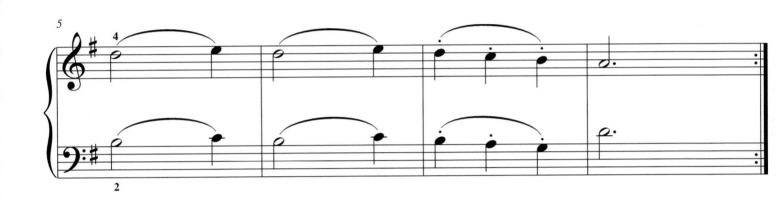

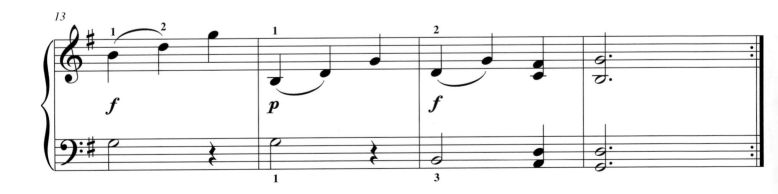

Menuet in F Major

Leopold Mozart
(1719–1787)

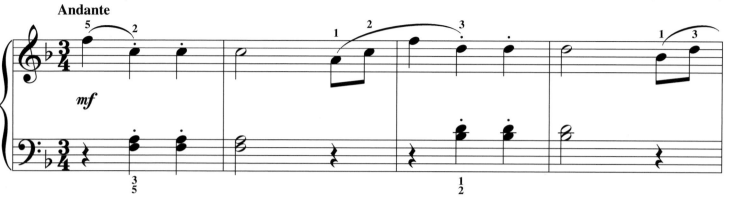

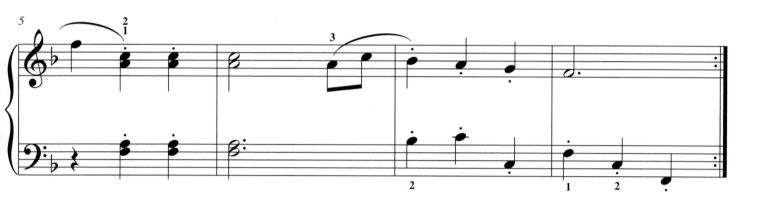

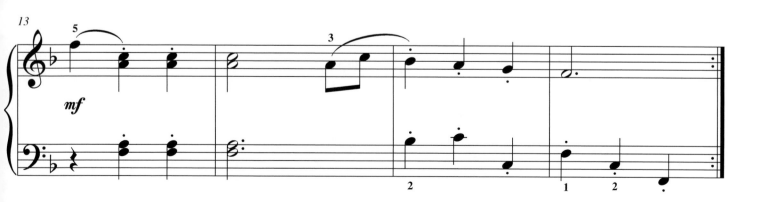

Trumpet Tune

William Duncombe
(1690-1769)

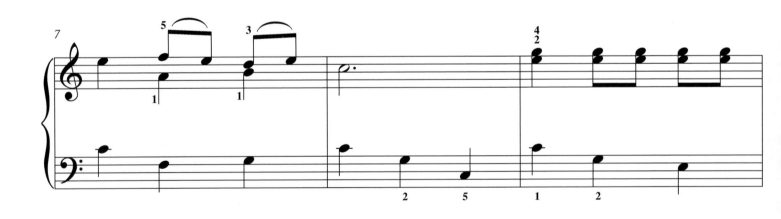

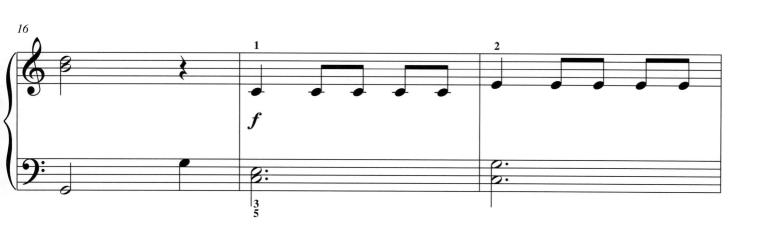

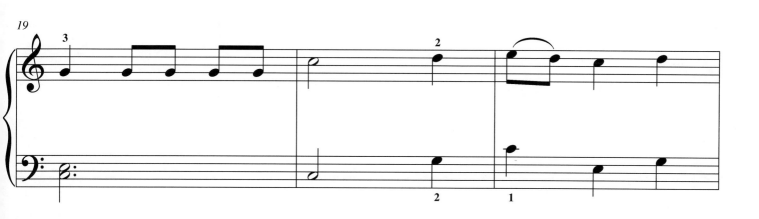

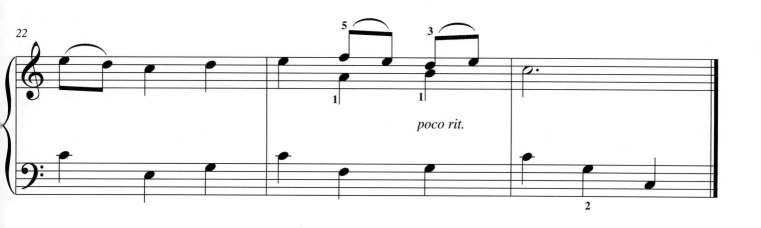

Waltz

Moritz Vogel
(1846–1922)

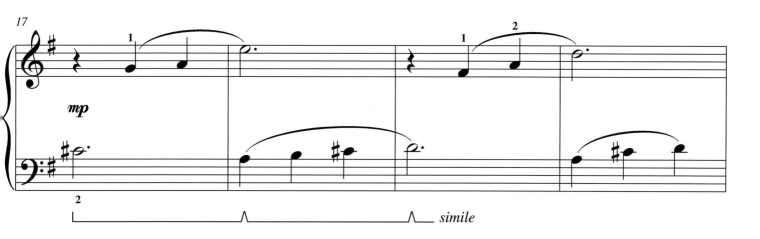

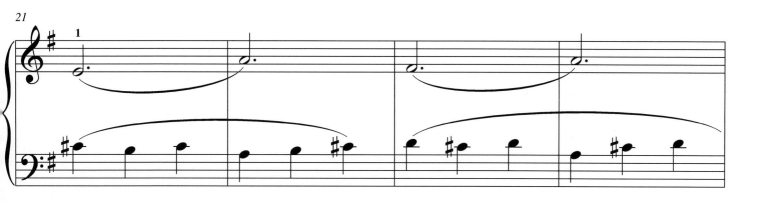

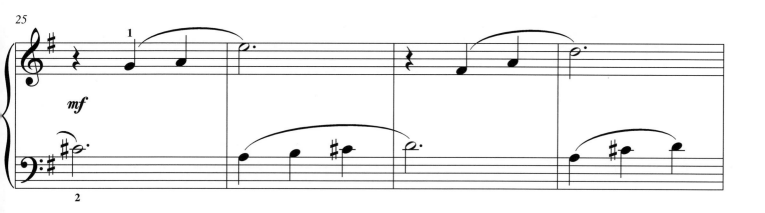

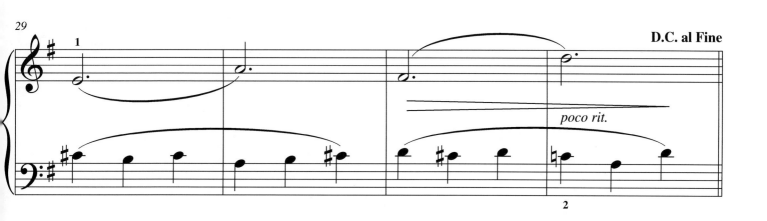

Little Sonata

I.

Charles H. Wilton
(1761–1832)

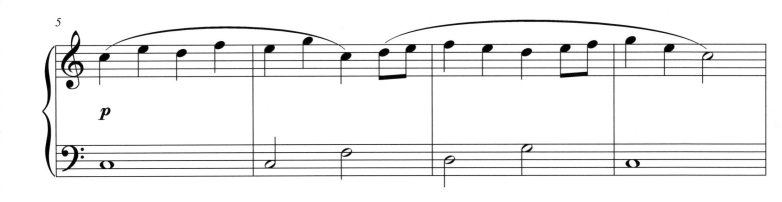

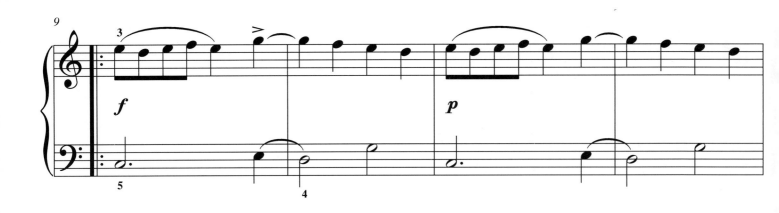

II.

Minuet

Melody

(Arabian Air)

Félix Le Couppey
(1811–1887)

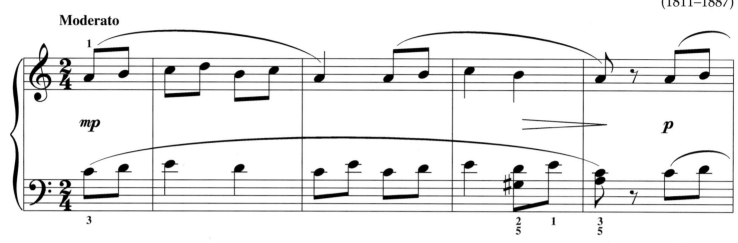

Minuet in G Major

BWV 822

Johann Sebastian Bach
(1685–1750)

Morning Prayer

Op. 101, No. 2

Cornelius Gurlitt
(1820–1901)

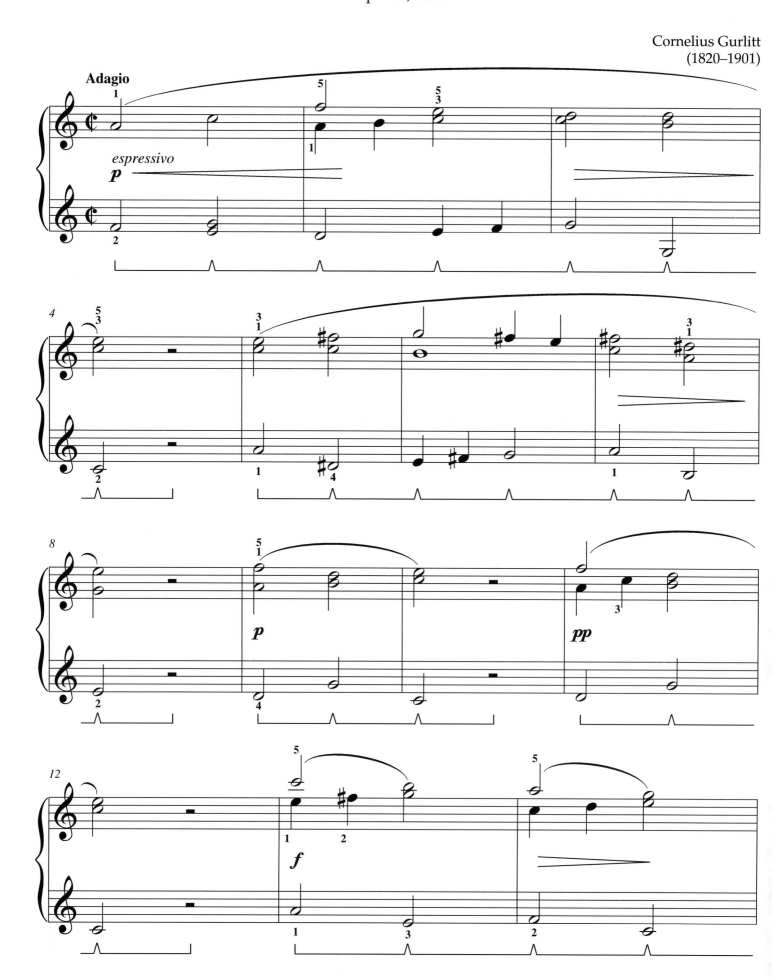

Bagatelle

Anton Diabelli
(1781–1858)

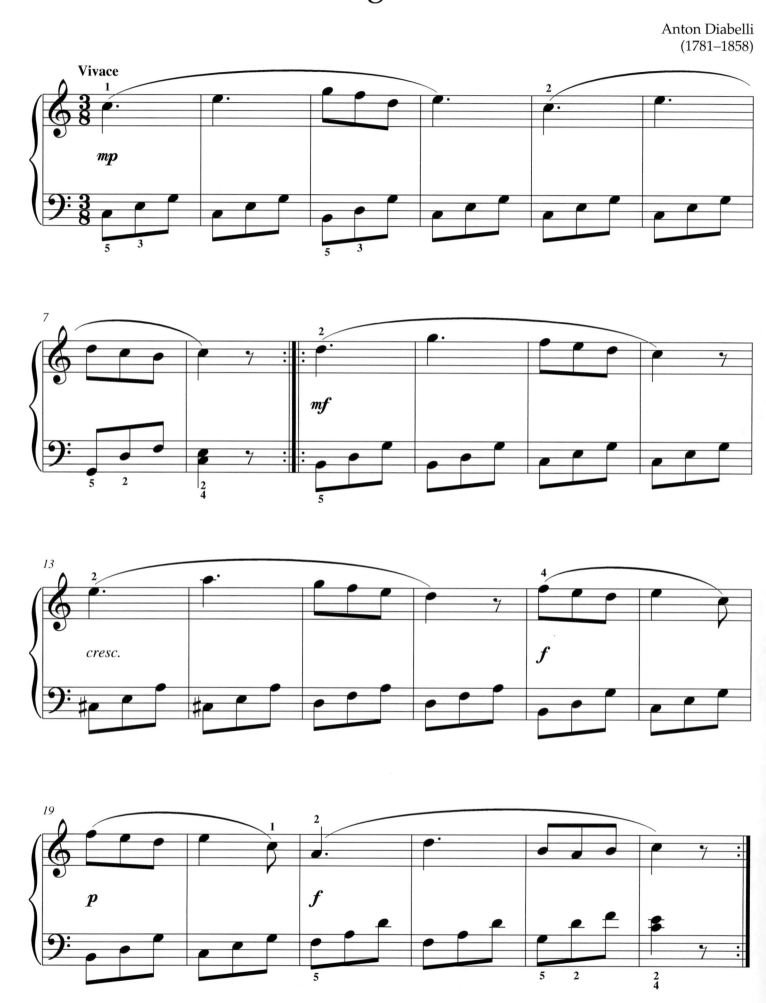

Tarantella
Op. 14, No. 8

Frank Lynes
(1858–1913)

Giga

Samuel Arnold
(1740–1802)

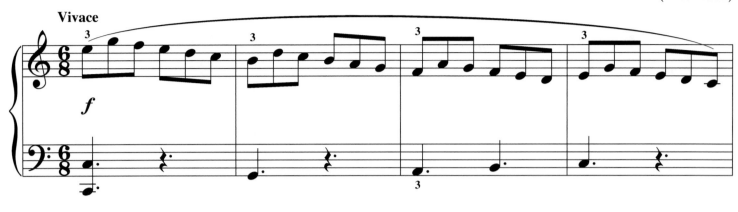

Musette

Félix Le Couppey
(1811-1887)

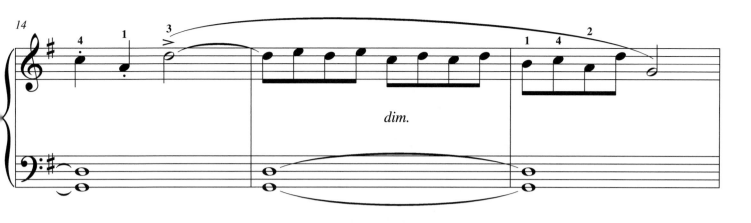

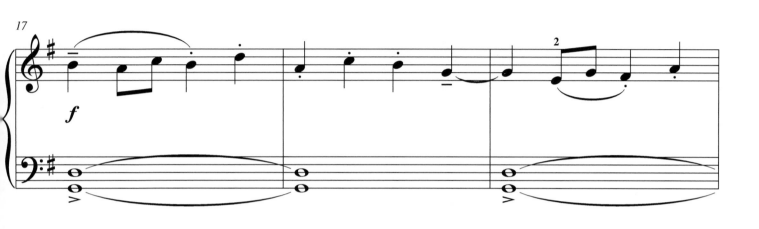

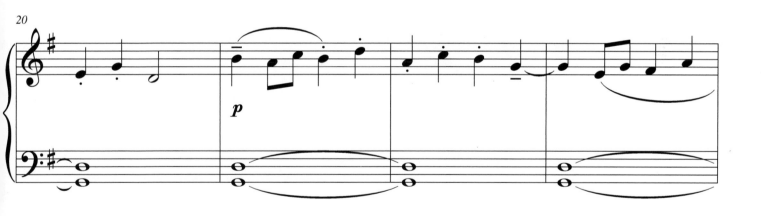

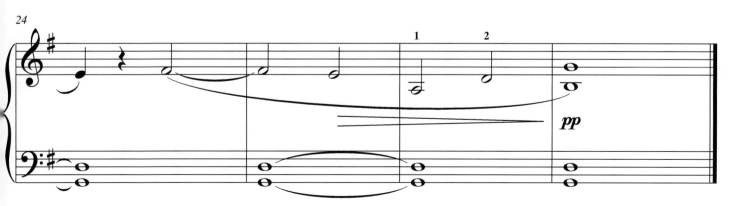

Scotch Dance

Friedrich Kuhlau
(1787–1832)

Burleske

Leopold Mozart
(1719-1787)

Menuet in G Major

Christian Petzold
(1677–1733)

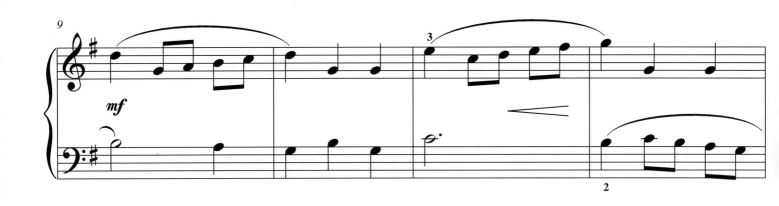

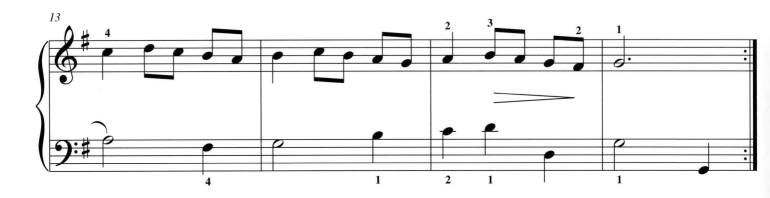

Menuet in F Major

Wolfgang Amadeus Mozart
(1756–1791)

Moderato

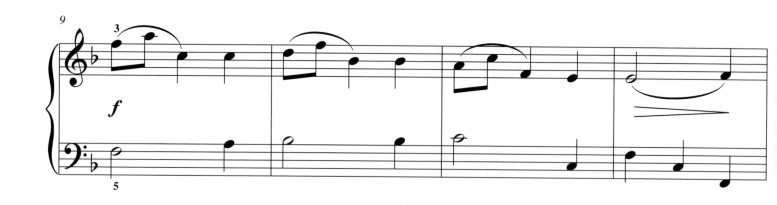

Church Bells

Matthew Camidge
(1758–1844)

Bright Sky
(Op. 140, No. 3)

Cornelius Gurlitt
(1820-1901)

Sad at Heart
Op. 47, No. 5

Robert Fuchs
(1847–1927)

Sarabande

Johann Pachelbel
(1653–1706)

Distant Bells

Op. 63, No. 6

Louis Streabbog
(1835-1886)

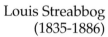

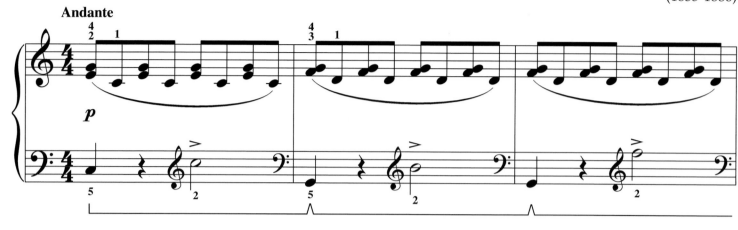

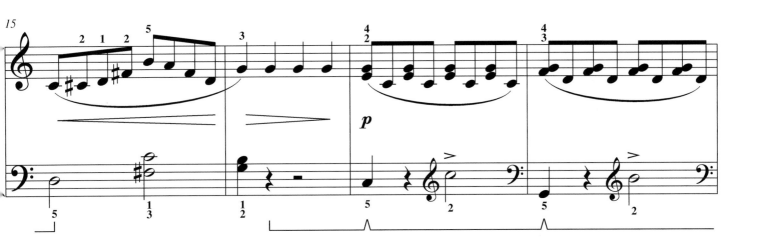

Night Escape
Op. 82, No. 65

Cornelius Gurlitt
(1820-1901)